Daily Prayers

Daily Prayers

RUBI MARTINEZ

Rubi Martinez
Daily Prayers

All rights reserved
Copyright © 2025 by **Rubi Martinez**

Published by Spines Publishing Platform
ISBN: 979-8-89691-548-5

Contents

Introduction

"PRAYERS TO EASE YOUR WORRIES:"

This prayer supports you every day and brings comfort during tough times.

I encourage you to revisit these prayers whenever you need peace or want to uplift your family in prayer.

Taking a few minutes each day to think about these words can help you find calm and strengthen your bond with your loved ones.

As mothers, wives, sisters, daughters, and friends, we should prioritize the spiritual development of our loved ones.

By encouraging them to cultivate a closer relationship with God and His Kingdom, we can help them establish a strong foundation for their journey through life.

Together, we can guide them toward a meaningful connection with their faith.

We need daily encouragement as wives, sisters, daughters, and friends.

Nurturing our relationship with God provides this support, helping us ground ourselves in faith and uplift others, thereby creating a loving environment.

The following are daily prayers that have proven beneficial in assisting me with my daily responsibilities, reflecting love and respect for all of us. Now, I am sharing them with you to help you be closer to God and to trust in Him.

Consider gifting this inspiring book to someone who could use a boost of motivation in their life, or simply share it with a good friend. It's the perfect way to uplift their spirits and show that you care!

Sincerely,

Rubi Martinez

PART ONE

Prayer for My Husband

One

Heavenly Father, I pray for my husband today.

Please protect him from harm and guide him away from danger, Give him good health, both physically and mentally.

Strengthen him when he feels weak, and comfort him when he is distressed.

Surround him with Your love and peace so he can feel Your presence every moment.

Strength and Courage:

Lord, I pray that You fill my husband with strength and courage as he faces life's challenges.

Grant him the resilience to overcome obstacles and remind him of his capabilities during moments of doubt. Help him remain steadfast in his beliefs and approach each day with renewed confidence and hope, knowing Your unwavering support is always with him.

For His Wisdom and Guidance:

Request for wisdom and guidance is made for the husband It is hoped that he will gain clarity of mind in decision-making and discernment in actions, a desire is expressed for him to follow a path aligned with a higher purpose; the intention is for him to seek guidance and trust in a designated direction.

For His Joy and Fulfillment:

Gracious God, I ask that You grant my husband happiness and contentment across all aspects of his life. May he experience fulfillment in his career, joy in his connections with others, and serenity in his spirit.

Guide him to see the blessings surrounding him and inspire him to embrace each day with thankfulness and intention.

For Your Relationship:

Lord, I ask for Your guidance in our relationship.

Fortify the connection between us, enhance our love, and assist us in communicating with openness and sincerity.

May we consistently be a source of support and solace for one another, and may our love mirror the love You have for us.

For his emotional and spiritual growth:

God, I ask that You bring my husband closer to You, open his heart to Your word, and deepen his understanding of Your love.

Help him grow in faith, patience, and compassion, when he faces doubts or struggles, remind him of Your unwavering support and the strength he can find in You.

Jeremiah 1:12

The Lord said to me, You have seen correctly, for I am watching to see that my word is fulfilled.

PART TWO

Prayer for My Wife

For Her Health and Well-Being:

Heavenly Father, please provide blessings of health and well-being to my wife.

Ensure her protection from illness and injury, and grant her strength and vitality, if she is experiencing any health challenges, may she receive healing and comfort.

Surround her with love and peace, enabling her to feel a sense of Your presence in all circumstances.

Loving God, I humbly ask that You envelop my wife's life in an abundance of joy and genuine happiness.

May she discover deep fulfillment in her passions, whether they are creative, personal, or professional, and experience profound joy in her relationships with family and friends.

Grant her a sense of tranquility that fills her heart, allowing her to appreciate the myriad of blessings surrounding her.

Help her to embrace each day with a spirit of gratitude and a clear sense of purpose, so she can navigate life's challenges with grace.

May her radiant smile illuminate our lives, and may her infectious laughter echo warmly throughout our home, creating a sanctuary of love and positivity.

For Her Wisdom and Guidance:

Heavenly Father, I humbly come before You, asking for Your divine wisdom and guidance to envelop my beloved wife.

Please grant her clarity of mind as she navigates her decisions, allowing her to see the path ahead with insightful understanding.

Bestow upon her the discernment needed in her actions, guiding her to make choices that align with Your perfect will.

Lead her along the unique journey "You" have prepared specifically for her, helping her to trust wholeheartedly in Your direction.

May she consistently seek your will in every aspect of her life and find deep comfort in the constant assurance of your presence surrounding her.

Proverbs 31:10-31:

This passage describes the virtuous woman and her qualities, highlighting her worth and the value she brings to her family.

A wife of noble character, who can find? She is worth far more than rubies.

Prayer for My Parents:

Ten

Heavenly Father, today I come before You with deep gratitude for my parents. I cherish the gift of their lives and all the love and sacrifices they have made for me.

I earnestly ask for Your divine protection to envelop them, shielding them from any illness and harm that may come their way.

Please grant them resilience and strength, both in their bodies and in their minds, to navigate the challenges they face; surround them with your calming peace, and if they encounter any health issues, I humbly pray for your healing touch to restore their well-being and your comforting presence to bring them solace.

Dear Lord, I come to You with a heartfelt prayer for my parents' emotional and spiritual well-being. Please fill their lives with abundant joy and deep contentment, allowing their hearts to overflow with Your comforting peace and unending love, If they are burdened by worries or anxieties, I ask that You wrap them in Your embrace, providing solace and strength to face their challenges.

Guide them to draw nearer to You, nourishing their faith and trust so they may experience the fullness of Your grace in their lives.

Dear God, I ask that you bestow upon my parents the profound wisdom and insight they need in every decision they face.

Grant them clarity of mind, allowing them to see beyond the surface and discern what is truly right and just in their actions, illuminating their path with your divine light, leading them toward the purpose you have designed for their lives.

May they find solace in your presence, trusting fully in your divine plan, and may they always feel your support guiding them through every challenge.

Heavenly Father, I humbly come before You to pray for the relationship between my parents, i ask that You strengthen the bond they share, allowing them to grow closer together each day.

May their love deepen, nurturing a connection that reflects trust, respect, and understanding.

Help them communicate openly and honestly with one another, fostering an environment where they can share their thoughts and feelings without fear of judgment, as challenges arise, grant them the wisdom and patience to navigate through their differences and come out stronger on the other side.

I pray that they continue to support and cherish each other, celebrating the joys of life together and leaning on each other during difficult times, may their love be a shining example of Your unwavering love for them, inspiring others to strive for the same. Amen.

If they are feeling lonely or isolated:

God, I lift up my parents to You, praying that You would bestow upon them the comfort of Your presence and surround them with Your boundless love, i ask that You facilitate connections with others, guiding them toward companionship and supportive relationships that lift their spirits and alleviate their sense of isolation.

Daniel 1:20

Praise be the name of God forever and ever and ever; wisdom and power are His Amen.

PART FOUR

Prayers for My Son:

Fourteen

Heavenly Father, I come before You with a heart full of love for my son, entrusting him to Your boundless grace and protection, i ask that You envelop him in Your loving embrace, providing him with a shield against any harm that might come his way, whether physical or emotional, surround him with your mighty angels, who will stand watch over him and guide his path, steering him away from danger and negativity, as he embarks on his daily journeys and pursuits, may your divine presence grant him safety and peace in every step he takes.

Heavenly Father,

I come before You with a heartfelt prayer for my son's health and well-being, please grant him the strength and vitality he needs in both body and mind to face the challenges of each day, wrap him in Your protective embrace, shielding him from illness, injury, and any harm that may come his way.

If he is currently experiencing health challenges or struggling with discomfort, I humbly ask for Your healing touch to restore him to health, providing him with comfort and peace during this time, help him to feel Your presence and know that he is never alone.

Guide him toward a life of balance and wellness in all aspects, including physical, emotional, and spiritual health, may he cultivate habits that nourish his body, foster resilience in his mind, and nurture his spirit.

Surround him with love, support, and positivity so that he may thrive and flourish. In Your name, I pray. Amen.

Gracious and loving God,

I come to you with a heartfelt plea, seeking your profound wisdom and gentle guidance for my son as he journeys through life, i earnestly ask that you bestow upon him an abundance of wisdom and discernment, empowering him to navigate the often tumultuous waters of decision-making, as he encounters various crossroads and choices, may he possess the clarity needed to align his actions with the unique purpose you have crafted for him.

In moments when uncertainty looms large and confusion sets in, I ask that you illuminate his path, casting away the shadows of doubt that may cloud him, allowing him to pause, reflect, and seek the stillness in his heart where he can hear your guiding voice.

Grant him the ability to recognize the signs you place in his life, allowing him to follow the direction that leads to fulfillment and joy.

Malachi 1:6,7

I, the Lord, do not change, so you, the descendants of Jacob, are not destroyed, ever since the time of your ancestors, you have turned away from my decrees and have not kept them, return to me, and I will return to you, says the Lord Almighty. Amen.

PART FIVE

Prayers for My Daughter

For her protection and safety:

Heavenly Father, I humbly place my precious daughter into Your loving and watchful care. I earnestly ask for Your divine protection to envelop her like a warm, comforting shield, guarding her from any harm that may come her way, both in body and spirit.

Guide her steps along the right paths, away from any lurking dangers and negativity she may encounter in her daily life.

Surround her with your heavenly angels, filling her heart and mind with a profound sense of peace and security that only you can provide.

For her health and well-being:

Lord, I come before You to lift up my daughter's health and to bestow upon her the strength and vitality she needs in her body, mind, and spirit, allowing her to flourish in every aspect of her life.

Safeguard her from illness and injury, and if she faces any health challenges, I beseech you to extend your healing touch and comforting presence.

May she find harmony and wellness in all areas of her life, experiencing the deep, abiding peace that flows from placing her trust in you.

For her wisdom and guidance:

God, I ask that You grant my daughter wisdom and discernment to make choices that honor You and align with Your purpose for her life.

Lead her on the right path and give her clarity of mind in times when she always seeks Your guidance and trusts in Your loving plan for her.

Heavenly Father, I come before You with a heartfelt prayer for my daughter's emotional and spiritual development.

I ask that You help her cultivate a deep sense of self-worth, grounded in the profound love You hold for her.

As she navigates the complexities of life, may her faith blossom, and may she embody compassion and understanding for herself and others.

In moments of sadness or feelings of loneliness, be her refuge and comfort, enveloping her in your tender care.

Fill her heart with an enduring sense of peace and joy that transcends circumstance.

May she always recognize how truly cherished and invaluable she is in Your eyes, fostering a spirit that radiates confidence and grace. Amen.

Heavenly Father,

Proverbs 3:5–6

Trust in the LORD with all your heart, and do not lean on your own understanding. In all your ways acknowledge Him, and He will make straight your paths.

PART SIX

Prayers for My Sister

Twenty

Heavenly Father, I come to You with a heavy heart as I lift my beloved sister up before You today.

I earnestly seek your divine protection to envelop her in a safe embrace, guarding her from any physical harm and emotional turmoil that may come her way.

Please illuminate her path with your wisdom, guiding her steps away from danger and leading her toward opportunities for growth and joy.

Surround her with your celestial angels, who can watch over her fiercely, providing comfort and strength in times of uncertainty.

Instill in her a profound sense of peace and security so that she may navigate her daily life with confidence and grace.

Fill her heart with your love, helping her to feel shielded and cherished in every situation i trust in your unfailing presence and protection over her, now and always. Amen.

Heavenly Father,

I come before you with a heartfelt prayer for my sister's health and well-being.

I ask that you fill her with strength, vitality, and energy in her body, mind, and spirit.

Surround her with your protection, keeping her safe from illness and injury.

If she is currently facing any health challenges, I humbly request your healing touch to bring her comfort and restoration.

Lord, please grant her the wisdom and insight to make choices that contribute to her overall wellness.

Help her find balance not just in her physical health, but also in her emotional and mental states, fostering a harmonious connection between her mind, body, and spirit.

May she be filled with positivity and resilience, enabling her to navigate life's hurdles with grace.

In moments of stress or uncertainty, may she experience the deep peace that comes from trusting in You and Your plan for her life.

Let her feel your love and support enveloping her, reminding her that she is never alone in her journey.

I pray that she flourishes in every facet of her life and that joy and health become her constant companions. Amen.

Exodus 15:26

He said, "If you listen carefully to the Lord your God and do what is right in His eyes, if you pay attention to His commands and keep all His decrees, I will not bring on you any of the disasters I brought on the Egyptians, for I am the Lord who heals you." Amen.

PART SEVEN

Prayers for My Brother

For His Relationships:

Dear God, I lift my brother's relationships to You in prayer.

Please surround him with a circle of genuine, loving friends who uplift him and support him through life's challenges.

Grant him the wisdom to nurture relationships that bring joy, encouragement, and laughter into his life.

Help him build meaningful connections that are based on mutual respect, understanding, and kindness.

Protect him from toxic influences and help him recognize those who may not have his best interests at heart.

May he find companionships that inspire him to grow, share, and celebrate life's moments together, fostering a bond that enriches his spirit and brings harmony to his life.

For His Future and Purpose:

Lord, I earnestly pray for my brother's future and the discovery of his unique purpose.

Illuminate his path and guide him in uncovering his true calling, showcasing the special gifts and talents You have bestowed upon him.

Fill him with the courage and confidence to chase his dreams fearlessly, even when faced with obstacles.

May he find fulfillment and joy in his endeavors, allowing his passions to shine and radiate to others as he navigates life's journey, may he use his abilities to make a positive impact on those around him, spreading your love and light in every aspect of his life.

Empower him to embrace opportunities, learn from experiences, and flourish into a remarkable person.

Help him to cultivate connections that are enriching and rewarding, filled with kindness and understanding. Guide him as he nurtures those bonds, ensuring that they bring out the best in him and inspire him to grow.

For His Future and Purpose:

Lord, I seek your guidance for my brother's future and the unfolding of his unique purpose. Illuminate his journey, helping him discover the paths that resonate with his true self and passions. Instill in him the confidence and resilience needed to pursue his dreams with determination, ensuring that he views challenges as opportunities for growth and learning.

In 2 Samuel 13:20,

Absalom, the brother of Tamar, inquires if Amnon, their other brother, has been with her. He advises Tamar to remain quiet about the incident, emphasizing the familial relationship.

PART EIGHT

Prayers for a Friend

For a friend who is struggling:

Dear God, in this moment of hardship, I ask You to wrap my dear friend [friend's name] in Your comforting embrace.

As they navigate through these challenging times, grant them a sense of strength to carry on, courage to face each new day, and a glimmer of hope to light their path.

Surround them with your everlasting love and support, reminding them that they are never alone. Amen.

For a friend who is sick:

Dear God, I come before You with a heavy heart, seeking Your divine healing for my beloved friend [friend's name]. Please ease their pain and discomfort and restore their body to health.

May they feel Your presence beside them, providing comfort in their suffering, and may each passing day bring them closer to full recovery. Amen.

For a friend who is celebrating:

Dear God, I thank You for the wonderful blessings that fill my friend [friend's name]'s life at this joyful moment their heart overflow with happiness and their spirit soar with delight. Amen.

Proverbs 27:10 advises you not to forsake your own friend or your father's friend during tough times. It also warns against going to your brother's house when you are in trouble; a helpful neighbor who is nearby can be better than a brother who lives far away.

PART NINE

Praying for our marriage:

Prayers for a Stronger Marriage

Dear God, we humbly come to You, seeking Your divine guidance and strength as we navigate the beautiful yet challenging journey of marriage.

Grant us the ability to communicate with honesty and openness so that we may understand each other's thoughts and feelings more deeply.

Help us to forgive one another without reservation, embracing a spirit of grace and understanding.

May our love be unconditional, flourishing with each passing day, and our bond grow ever stronger, deeply rooted in trust. Respect and an unwavering commitment to one another. Amen.

Prayers for Unity in Marriage:

Dear God, we approach You with hopeful hearts, yearning for unity in our marriage.

Help us become one in heart, mind, and purpose, harmonizing our lives and dreams.

Grant us the wisdom to tackle our conflicts with patience and understanding, approaching each disagreement as an opportunity for growth may Instill in us the humility needed to admit our faults and the grace to forgive each other, May our love embody the essence of Your love—selfless, patient, and kind—shining brightly in our lives and in the world around us. Amen.

Prayers for Healing in Marriage:

Dear God, we earnestly seek Your healing touch upon our marriage.

Where there is pain and hurt, bring Your gentle comfort to soothe our souls.

Where there is anger and frustration, fill our hearts with peace.

Help us to let go of past grievances and extend forgiveness, allowing us to rebuild the trust that has been shaken.

May your boundless love rejuvenate our relationship, enabling us to rise from the ashes of discord even stronger than before. Amen.

Prayers for a Struggling Marriage:

Dear God, we come to You in our time of need, our hearts heavy with the burdens of a struggling marriage. We acknowledge the difficulties we face and humbly ask for Your guidance and intervention.

Grant us the strength to persevere through the trials ahead and the courage to seek help when needed. Bestow upon us the wisdom to recognize the necessary changes we must make for healing and growth.

May your everlasting love illuminate our path, guiding us back to each other and reigniting the spark of love we once cherished Amen.

Marriage is a respected and valued commitment that plays a vital role in our lives, It represents a partnership built on trust, love, and mutual respect.

The intimacy shared within marriage is a sacred bond that should be nurtured and protected, creating a space that is pure and meaningful.

Upholding these values is essential, as they foster a healthy and supportive it's important to recognize the consequences of actions that undermine this sacred commitment, such as infidelity or promiscuity, By promoting fidelity and honoring the sanctity of marriage, we contribute to a healthier society and cultivate stronger relationships.

Deuteronomy 11:11

Love the Lord your God and keep His requirements, His decrees, His laws, and His commands always Amen.

PART TEN

Prayers for Specific Situations:

Prayers for Anger:

Lord, I come before You with a heavy heart, burdened by the anger that often overtakes my spirit.

I ask for your divine assistance in releasing this frustration that consumes me.

Please envelop me in your calming peace and gently guide me toward the path of forgiveness.

Teach me to respond with kindness and empathy, even when faced with challenging circumstances.

May your grace enable me to show compassion where it is most needed Amen.

Heavenly Father, I acknowledge my shortcomings and confess that I have let my anger lead me astray.

I seek your forgiveness for my actions and words that have been rooted in this anger.

Please help me to find the strength to forgive those who have caused me pain.

Heal the deep wounds that fuel my resentment and replace them with your unconditional love.

May your light shine through me as I learn to let go and embrace peace Amen.

When Feeling Anger Rising:

Lord, I sense the tide of anger swelling within me, threatening to overwhelm my thoughts and actions.

In this moment, I ask for your guidance to take a step back and breathe deeply, allowing your calming presence to wash over me.

Grant me the wisdom to respond thoughtfully rather than to react impulsively.

Please help me cultivate the self-control needed to navigate this emotion with grace. Amen.

When Wronged by Someone:

Lord, my heart is heavy with hurt and anger due to the actions I feel the weight of this pain, and it is difficult to move past it.

I come to you seeking strength and the ability to forgive, just as you have so generously forgiven me.

Heal the wounds in my heart, Lord, and help me to release the anger that has taken hold of me, freeing me from its grasp. Amen.

When Struggling with Resentment:

Lord, I acknowledge that I have been clinging to feelings of resentment that cloud my heart and mind.

Amen.

Psalm 91:1

Whoever dwells in the shelter of the Most High will rest in the shadow of the Almighty Amen.

Prayers for Anxiety

Dear God, in this moment of deep introspection, I am acutely aware of the burden of anxiety that feels as though it is pressing heavily upon my chest, constricting my breath and clouding my mind.

My thoughts rush chaotically like a relentless storm, each wave bringing with it a new worry, making it nearly impossible to find any sense of clarity or calm.

The tension in my muscles is palpable, leaving me feeling restless and on edge, unable to find peace in my surroundings.

I earnestly seek your divine peace, a profound tranquility that transcends our understanding, to wash over me like a gentle tide, bringing comfort to my troubled spirit.

Please calm my racing thoughts, soothe my fears, and help me to refocus on Your unwavering love and eternal care that surrounds me. Amen.

Lord, at this moment in time, I find myself deeply engulfed by feelings of anxiety and fear that seem to permeate my every thought.

This overwhelming uncertainty leaves me seeking your reassurance and comfort in these times of distress.

Help me to remember that you are an ever-present companion in my life, a constant source of strength and support upon which I can lean without hesitation.

Grant me the inner fortitude to confront my fears directly and the courage to rise above the challenges they present.

Fill my heart with your soothing peace and instill in me a renewed sense of hope that acts as a guiding light in the darkness, illuminating the path I must take. Amen.

Heavenly Father, I humbly come before You, ready to lay down the heavy anxieties I carry, as if placing burdens far too great for me at Your feet.

I trust wholly in Your sovereignty and divine plan.

Knowing that you are in complete control of all things—both those that I can see and those that remain hidden.

Help me to release my worries and anxieties, allowing them to drift away as I embrace the peace that comes from entrusting my life to You.

Grant me the serenity to accept those things in life that I cannot change, the courage to take purposeful action where I can make a difference, and the wisdom to discern between the two.

May I find comfort in knowing that every challenge is an opportunity for growth under your guidance Amen.

Psalm 94:18-19

18: When I said, my foot is sleeping, your unfailing love, LORD, supported me.

19: When anxiety was great within me, your consolation brought me joy. Amen.

Prayers for Peace

Dear God, I humbly come before You in this challenging moment, earnestly seeking Your divine peace and comfort.

I appreciate your presence and guidance during this difficult time.

The weight of my burdens feels almost insurmountable, and my heart is heavy with worry.

My thoughts are in turmoil, spiraling through waves of anxiety and uncertainty that seem to cloud my vision of hope.

I confidently call upon you, Lord, to grant me your extraordinary peace, one that surpasses all understanding. Calm my restless fears and soothe my troubled mind, enveloping me in your infinite love that knows no limits.

Help me to recognize your presence in my life, guiding me through the shadows toward the light. Amen.

Dear Lord, as I find myself weary and heavily laden with worries that feel like an insidious weight on my spirit, I seek Your comforting embrace.

In this moment of distress, I yearn for your presence to fill me with the journey of life.

I invite you to surround me with your loving support, creating a sense of security that empowers me to grow and thrive.

Grant me the strength to recognize that support and encouragement are vital forces in overcoming life's challenges.

These nurturing elements act as a comforting reminder that, even in our darkest moments, we are not alone in our struggles.

This unwavering support cultivates a deep sense of hope and resilience within us, enabling us to imagine a future brimming with promise and joy.

Such encouragement becomes indispensable during trying times, inspiring us to navigate life's obstacles with courage and fostering a sense of optimism for the brighter days that await us on the horizon.

Psalm 93:1

The LORD reigns; He is robed in majesty and armed with strength; indeed, the world is established, firm, and secure. Amen.

PART ELEVEN

Prayers for Divorce:

Prayers for Healing and Strength Through a Divorce

Dear God, my heart feels shattered, and I find myself wandering in a fog of confusion and despair as I endure this challenging divorce.

I humbly ask for your strength to navigate this painful journey and the courage to embrace whatever the future holds.

Please heal the deep emotional wounds that weigh heavily on my soul and guide me toward a place of peace and healing. Amen.

Lord, the overwhelming pain and uncertainty of this divorce are suffocating.

I seek refuge in your unwavering support and the faith to trust your divine plan for my life.

Please grant me the wisdom to make thoughtful and fair decisions during this tumultuous time, and the strength to forge ahead with renewed hope and purpose. Amen.

Heavenly Father, I find myself grappling with intense emotions of anger, sadness, and confusion that swirl within me.

Please wrap me in your comforting embrace during this distressing period and help me cultivate forgiveness, both for myself and for others who have played a part in this journey.

Grant me the serenity to accept the things in my life that are beyond my control, giving me the peace to let go of frustrations and worries.

May I find the courage and determination to take action in the areas where I can make a difference, working tirelessly toward improvement.

Help me develop a keen discernment that allows me to recognize and understand the difference between what I can change and what I must simply accept. Amen.

Lord, as I navigate the important choices and crossroads that lie ahead, I ask for clarity of mind that cuts through confusion and sharp discernment to assess each situation accurately.

Please guide me in focusing on the decisions that will bring forth the greatest benefits for both myself and my family, Instill in me a deep and unwavering trust in Your guidance, helping me to have faith at each moment, knowing that with Your support, I can face whatever challenges may arise. Amen.

Psalm 100:4, 5

4: Enter the gates with thanksgiving and his courts with praise; give thanks to him and praise his name. 5: For the LORD is good, and his love endures forever. Amen.

PART TWELVE

Prayers for Addiction:

Embracing Strength and Hope on the Path to Recovery

The journey through addiction can feel overwhelming and daunting, encompassing a range of times, the power of prayer can provide a source of comfort, resilience, and hope for individuals striving to reclaim their lives, Below are some heartfelt prayers that address different facets of the recovery process, each designed to inspire courage and determination.

For Strength and Courage:

Dear God, I humbly come before You, yearning for the strength and courage necessary to confront my addiction.,(mention whatever addiction you need prayer for) In moments of weakness and despair, I often feel lost and shackled by the very thing I wish to escape.

Yet, I believe that with Your divine guidance and love, I can discover the fortitude to resist temptation and liberate myself from this painful cycle.

Please grant me the resolve to move forward and embrace a life filled with purpose. Amen.

Lord, as I stand on the precipice of this challenging journey, fear often grips my heart, and the obstacles ahead seem insurmountable.

Nevertheless, I find comfort in the knowledge that you walk alongside me, supporting my every step. Please endow me with the courage to confront my fears, the resilience to persevere through hardship, and the steadfast determination to remain committed to my recovery.

With your guidance and wisdom:

Lord, I find myself in a state of confusion and uncertainty, torn between the pull of my addiction and the yearning for a better life.

I humbly ask for Your guidance to help me navigate through this challenging time.

Please lead me to the resources and support systems that can assist me in overcoming this struggle.

Grant me the wisdom to make choices that reflect a commitment to my health and well-being, and the inner strength to resist the harmful influences that seek to drag me back into darkness.

Dear God, as I seek to break free from the chains of my addiction, I ask for Your help in identifying the specific triggers that exacerbate my cravings.

Illuminate my mind so that I may develop healthy coping strategies to handle stress and emotional pain.

I pray for clarity in my thoughts, allowing me to make sound decisions that align with my goal of recovery, and for the strength to resist temptation whenever it arises. Amen.

For Healing and Wholeness:

Lord, I stand before You, feeling broken and in desperate need of Your healing touch.

Psalm 41:3

The LORD sustains them on their sickbed and restores them from their bed of illness. Amen.

PART THIRTEEN

Prayers for Mindset:

General Prayers for Mindset:

Dear God, I come to You with a humble heart, seeking a positive and healthy mindset that can enable me to live my life to the fullest.

Please help me release the negative thoughts and limiting beliefs that have been weighing me down.

Fill my mind with Your divine peace, unshakeable joy, and unwavering hope.

Grant me the strength to cultivate a mindset that sees the good in all situations and allows me to approach each day with renewed optimism. Amen.

Lord, I desire to cultivate a mind that is open to the vast array of possibilities and opportunities that life presents.

Help me to rise above fear and doubt, which often hold me captive.

Encourage me to embrace challenges, viewing them as opportunities for growth, and to face them with unwavering courage and confidence.

May I remember that, with Your support, I can conquer the obstacles in my path and step into a future filled with potential. Amen.

Heavenly Father,

I come before You seeking Your wisdom and guidance in developing a mindset rooted in gratitude and appreciation.

Help me shift my focus toward the positive aspects of my life, recognizing the countless blessings that surround me.

Teach me to identify and celebrate the little joys in each moment, no matter how small they may seem.

May I learn to express my gratitude freely, allowing it to transform my outlook and fill my heart with happiness each day. Amen.

Prayers for Specific Mindset Challenges:

For Overcoming Fear and Anxiety:

Lord, I come before You, burdened by fear and anxiety that often cloud my mind and hinder my daily life.

In moments when my heart races and my thoughts spiral out of control, I seek your comforting presence.

Please help me trust in your unwavering love and find solace in your embrace.

Grant me the courage to confront my fears head-on and the strength to rise above them, knowing that You are by my side. Amen.

For Developing Self-Discipline:

Dear Lord, I find myself struggling with self-discipline, feeling adrift in my pursuits and goals.

Please help me cultivate the focus, determination, and perseverance necessary to stay on track, especially when distractions arise.

Grant me the strength to resist temptation and to make choices that align with my aspirations and well-being.

Let your guidance be my anchor as I work toward achieving my dreams. Amen.

For Cultivating a Growth Mindset:

Gracious Lord, I desire to embrace challenges as valuable opportunities for growth, but I often feel shackled by limiting beliefs.

Psalm 20:1:

May the LORD answer you when you are in distress; may the name of the God of Jacob protect you. Amen.

About the Editor of This Book

Rubi grew up in Texas and discovered her inspiration for prayer and writing many years ago when she faced the stark realities of life.

Understanding that Jesus is the ultimate source of salvation, she and her family have navigated numerous challenges, including issues related to drugs, domestic violence, and alcohol.

Her household was often marked by a lack of respect and domestic violence, yet she remained committed to fulfilling her responsibilities as a mother to her three young sons.

Now, as a proud grandmother of five, she seeks to share the profound love of God with her family.

This motivation led her to write this book, in which she shares effective prayers to provide "peace for the soul."

I extend my gratitude to my fellow readers, and I hope this book serves as a valuable resource for your daily prayers.

Please remember that Jesus is always with us.

Thank you for your support.

God bless you all